I0009902

YOUR KNOWLEDGE HAS ...

- We will publish your bachelor's and master's thesis, essays and papers

- Your own eBook and book - sold worldwide in all relevant shops

- Earn money with each sale

Upload your text at www.GRIN.com
and publish for free

Bibliographic information published by the German National Library:

The German National Library lists this publication in the National Bibliography; detailed bibliographic data are available on the Internet at http://dnb.dnb.de .

Imprint:

Copyright © 2017 GRIN Verlag, Open Publishing GmbH
Print and binding: Books on Demand GmbH, Norderstedt Germany
ISBN: 9783668597730

This book at GRIN:

https://www.grin.com/document/384237

Hari KC

Smart Restaurant. A Management Application for Restaurants and Hotels

GRIN Publishing

GRIN - Your knowledge has value

Since its foundation in 1998, GRIN has specialized in publishing academic texts by students, college teachers and other academics as e-book and printed book. The website www.grin.com is an ideal platform for presenting term papers, final papers, scientific essays, dissertations and specialist books.

Visit us on the internet:

http://www.grin.com/

http://www.facebook.com/grincom

http://www.twitter.com/grin_com

SMART RESTAURANT

ABSTRACT

Traditional method that is commonly been used in hotels is by taking the customer's orders and writing it down on a piece of paper. Many solutions have been proposed for solving this issue. "Smart Restaurant" is a Management Application for ordering, browsing, searching and booking the hotel and restaurant services, menus and items. This Project aims to make easy for hotel services with minimum manpower and by digital in hotel.

No login or user authentication is required to view or search products. Any normal guest user can view on our services and view items and products inside hotel Wi-Fi coverage area and by web application. He/she can search/order different products and can even add them to the KOT also booking services then registered their basic info as Table Number using application by scanning the barcode on table.

We are implementing this system using Web application for User and Restaurant. There is an enormous potential benefit for these businesses in recording customer orders and serving the foods. Without any doubt this is very convenient, effective and easy so that it improves the performance of restaurant's staff and maximize the customer's visits which will ultimately boost the economy of the restaurant.

TABLE OF CONTENTS

LIST OF FIGURES

LIST OF TABLES

LIST OF ABBREVIBIATION

CRUD = Create Read Update Delete

RDBMS = Relational Database Management System

RGB = Red Blue Green

CMYK = Cyan Magenta Yellow Key

ER = Entity Relationship

SSD = System Sequence Diagram

UML = Unified Modeling Language

ACL = Access Control List

RBAC = Role Based Access Control

B2C = Business to Customers

CoD = Cash on Delivery

IoC = Inversion of Control

Chapter 1

INTRODUCTION

1.1. BACKGROUND

Popularity of restaurants has increased in recent years. The general practice in a restaurant involves the customer making his order and waiting for the ordered meal. However, the complaints received from customers regarding services offered in restaurants has increased too. This feeling of dissatisfaction is caused by many reasons, namely, delay in delivering customer's order. Advancement in communication technologies can be used to resolve these issues. Accordingly, this removing the limitations in the food ordering process, with the help of an integrated and networked system. This application involves the use of mobile phones for undertaking the food ordering process in restaurants.

Nowadays web services technology is widely used to integrate heterogeneous systems and develop new applications. Here an application of integration of hotel management systems by web services technology is presented. Smart Restaurant integrates lots of systems of hotel industry such as Ordering System Kitchen Order Ticket (KOT), Billing System and various services booking. This integration solution can add or expand hotel software system in any size of hotel chains environment.

This system increases quality and speed of service. This system also increases attraction of place for large range of customers. Implementing this system gives a cost-efficient opportunity to give your customers a personalized service experience where they are in control choosing what they want – from dining to ordering to payment and feedback.

1.2. PROBLEM STATEMENT

Traditionally the method in which customers specify their desired menu to the waiter who takes the order on a paper. Personally, he then takes the order to the kitchen department and then he supply the food item to the customer. So, it was a time-consuming process. It leads to wastage of paper and also it requires reprinting of all menu cards. Also, in many cases for small change to be making in menu card it is not convenient to print all menu cards again and again. Simply saying that the menu card once printed can't be changed. After some days, the menu card lost its worthy look and attractiveness.

Many of the hotel are managed their workflow and services by paper work and manually which take time and high budget for management. busy day of people schedule and value of time become important day by day so Smart Restaurant handle the system as booking and ordering by digitally which become save manpower and time of staff of hotel. Generating KOT by application is easy to save paper, staff and time. The hotel are services and facilized in a traditional way, from waiters to kitchen also on account. More recently, these system is one of the major problem for hotel to manage their manpower and guests.

1.3. OBJECTIVES

1.3.1. Primary Objectives

The main objective of this project is to make the ordering system of restaurant digital and effective. People would not have to wait for ordering the food and any kind of booking services which will be eliminating delay in services.

Features:

- To provide a feature rich for Digital KOT service
- To provide efficient management of users divided in 3 general categories as Guest User, Waiters/kitchen and Account.
- To build a feature rich for Automatic billing.
- To provide efficient Kitchen Display of KOT

1.3.2. Secondary Objectives

- To enable guest to search and view the menus of hotel and their restaurant.
- To provide a platform itself being a select and order the menus and book services.

1.4. IMPLICATION

This Project aims to provide services and hospitality by digitally in the hotel area. There are already a couple of hotel management site and application for ordering and booking services in Hotel. But Smart Restaurant would be a first in its kind and a unique application to mainly focus on the guest and staff of hotel. For a developing country like ours where the literacy rate is below the average, this project might help the hotel owner, manager and supervision to get/server their better service to their Customers onto a platform that really is built for one and only them.

There is a great necessity of such apps that would collaborate to reduce the management risk and promote the hotel. This project aims to provide a platform where people can view, search and order at a very effective and easy manner without any hard processes and tedious payment gateways. So, it must be a great concern to build such a product like this project.

4

Chapter 2

LITERATURE REVIEW

There are many billing and accounting software available in market being used in the hotel and restaurant sector, and most commonly we find the software called "Swastik Restaurant ERP", ALICE, ChowNow.

Swastik Restaurant ERP, is a desktop based Restaurant Management Software which is designed to provide restaurants all the features and tools which is required for smooth order, Billing, Operation, Accounting and Management. It is highly customized and User-Friendly Software that is used for any restaurant type including fine dining restaurants, fast food chains, cafes, bars, etc.

ALICE features both department-specific apps (Staff, Guest, and Concierge) as well as an overarching suite you can use for better operating efficiency across your property. With ALICE Staff, users can expect features such as internal messaging to keep in touch with staff members as well as the ability to manage and assign tickets. ALICE Concierge is helpful for those at the front desk, enabling employees to integrate your property management system to access important guest information and allowing you to track all requests within one system, including incidents, reservations, transportation services, wake-up calls, and more.

What's most exciting about this app is its Guest component, where guests can voice their needs and desires, giving them real-time status updates and notifications on the progress of a particular service. Guest tracking metrics are also available on all requests and reservations. ALICE is available for both iOS and Android operating systems.

ChowNow is online food ordering system that includes Facebook ordering, smart phone and web based ordering. This application is mainly developed to assist the customer where any customer can order food online and can take advantage of food delivery and take out features. ChowNow apps provides the credit card payment options and payment is transferred to bank accounts.

Chapter 3

TOOLS AND METHODOLOGY

3.1. REQUIRED TOOLS

The system is developed using the following tools:

3.1.1 Language

- JavaScript

JavaScript is a high-level, dynamic, untyped, and interpreted programming language which is used alongside HTML and CSS. JavaScript is easy to learn easy to edit and prototyping language easy to debug object oriented scripting language which allows you to create highly responsive interfaces that improve the user experience and provide dynamic functionality, without having to wait for the server to react and show another page. (wikipedia, https://en.wikipedia.org/wiki/JavaScript, 2016)

- Python

Python is a dynamically typed programming language designed by Guido Van Rossum. Much like the programming language Ruby, Python was designed to be easily read by programmers. Because of its large following and many libraries, Python can be implemented and used to do anything from webpages to scientific research. Python features a dynamic type system and automatic memory management and supports multiple programming paradigms, including object-oriented, imperative, functional programming, and procedural styles. It has a large and comprehensive standard library.

Python interpreters are available for many operating systems, allowing Python code to run on a wide variety of systems. Python, the reference implementation of Python, is open source software and has a community-based development model, as do nearly all of its variant implementations. Python is managed by the non-profit Python Software Foundation.

3.1.2 Framework

- Django

Django is a free and open source web application framework, written in Python. A web framework is a set of components that helps you to develop websites faster and easier. When you're building a website, you always need a similar set of components: a way to handle user authentication (signing up, signing in, signing out), a management panel for your website, forms, a way to upload files, etc.

Luckily for you, other people long ago noticed that web developers face similar problems when building a new site, so they teamed up and created frameworks (Django being one of them) that give you ready-made components to use. Frameworks exist to save you from having to reinvent the wheel and to help alleviate some of the overhead when you're building a new site.

- Vue.js

Vue.js (commonly referred to as Vue; pronounced   is an open Source progressive JavaScript   framework   for   building user interfaces. Integration into projects that use other JavaScript libraries is made easy with Vue because it is designed to be incrementally adoptable. Vue can also function as a web application framework capable of powering advanced single-page-application.

3.1.3 Software

- WebStorm

WebStorm is lightweight yet powerful Integrated Development Environment perfectly equipped for complex client-side development and server-side development with Node.js.

WebStorm features advanced support for JavaScript, HTML, CSS and their modern successors, as well as for frameworks such as AngularJS or React, debugging, and integration with the VCS and various web development tools:

Intelligent Editor with coding assistance for JavaScript, Node.js, ECMAScript 6, TypeScript, CoffeeScript, and Dart as well as HTML, CSS, Less, Sass and Stylus. Coding assistance includes syntax highlighting, documentation lookup, and refactoring's.

- ✓ On-the-fly code analysis, error highlighting, and quick fixes.
- ✓ Powerful navigation across the project and advanced refactoring's.
- ✓ Support for modern frameworks: AngularJS, React, Meteor, Express and more.
- ✓ Built-in debugger for the client-side code and Node.js.
- ✓ Integration with the build tools (Grunt, Gulp), code quality tools (JSHint, JSLint, ESLint, JSCS), test runners (Karma, Mocha) and VCS (Git, GitHub, Mercurial, SVN).
- ✓ VCS Integrations: out-of-the-box support for Subversion, Perforce, Git, and CVS with change lists and merge.

- Adobe Photoshop

Adobe Photoshop is a raster graphics editor for Windows and OS X. It can edit and compose raster images in multiple layers and supports

9

masks, alpha compositing and several color models including RGB, CMYK, Lab color space, spot color and duotone.

3.1.4 Version Control and Project Management

- Git and GitHub

Git is a free and open source distributed version control system designed to handle everything from small to very large projects with speed and efficiency. It is a distributed revision control system with an emphasis on speed, data integrity, and support for distributed, non-linear workflows.

GitHub is a Web-based Git version control repository hosting service. It is mostly used for Computer Code It offers all of the distributed version control and source code management (SCM) functionality of Git as well as adding its own features. It provides access control and several collaboration features such as bug tracking, feature request, task management and wikis for every project. GitHub offers both plans for private and free repositories on the same account which are commonly used to host open-sources software projects. As of April 2017, GitHub reports having almost 20 million users and 57 million repositories, making it the largest host of source code in the world.

3.2. ALGORITHM OR SOLUTION APPROACH USED

3.2.1 Role base access control

Role-based access control (RBAC) is an approach to restricting system access to authorized users. It is used by the majority of enterprises and can implement mandatory access control (MAC) or discretionary access control (DAC). RBAC is sometimes referred to as role-based security.

Role-based-access-control (RBAC) is a policy neutral access control mechanism defined around roles and privileges. The components of RBAC such as role-permissions, user-role and role-role relationships make it simple to perform user assignments. RBAC can be used to facilitate administration of security in large organizations with hundreds of users and thousands of permissions. Although RBAC is different from MAC and DAC access control frameworks, it can enforce these policies without any complication. Its popularity is evident from the fact that many products and businesses are using it directly or indirectly.

Within an organization, roles are created for various job functions. The permissions to perform certain operations are assigned to specific roles. System users are assigned particular roles, and through those role assignments acquire the computer permissions to perform particular computer-system functions. Since users are not assigned permissions directly, but only acquire them through their role (or roles), management of individual user rights becomes a matter of simply assigning appropriate roles to the user's account; this simplifies common operations, such as adding a user, or changing a user's department. (Wikipedia, 2016)

Three primary rules are defined for RBAC:

Role assignment: A subject can exercise a permission only if the subject has selected or been assigned a role.

Role authorization: A subject's active role must be authorized for the subject. With rule 1 above, this rule ensures that users can take on only roles for which they are authorized.

Permission authorization: A subject can exercise a permission only if the permission is authorized for the subject's active role. With rules 1 and 2, this rule ensures that users can exercise only permissions for which they are authorized.

Additional constraints may be applied as well, and roles can be combined in a hierarchy where higher-level roles subsume permissions owned by sub-roles.

3.2.2 Business to consumer model

B2C, or business-to-consumer, is the type of commerce transaction in which businesses sell products or services to consumers. Traditionally, this could refer to individuals shopping for clothes for themselves at the mall, diners eating in a restaurant, or subscribing to pay-per-view TV at home. More recently, the term B2C refers to the online selling of products, or e-tailing, in which manufacturers or retailers sell their products to consumers over the Internet.

The mid-1990s to the 2000s saw the rise of e-commerce through sites like Amazon, Zappos and Victoria's Secret. Now, it's rare to see a consumer-based business not sell their products online. Consumers enjoy the convenience of online shopping in their own homes, while businesses thrive on the low overhead. With a virtual storefront, a business doesn't need a storefront or a large inventory stocked at all times. This is ideal for small businesses, like a jewelry company or a bakery.

There are challenges for businesses in B2C, however. As websites continue to become flashier and more user-friendly, it's up to the business to keep their site intuitive and easy to navigate. The site must also be optimized to get consumer traffic — search engine marketing (SEM) is a necessity. Most consumers use search engines like Google, Bing and Yahoo! to find the products that they are looking to purchase. Customers generally choose websites on the first few pages of results after they've searched a specific keyword or phrase. If a site does not have a site with good SEM, they could get buried in the mix, lose site traffic, and thus lose potential customers.

Another challenge is the payment processing. SSL encryption lets people know that the site isn't compromised, but many people are hesitant to submit their credit cards to companies. Even if the site is safe, the place where the credit card numbers are stored is not. In 2004, the Payment Card Industry Security Standards Council (PCI) formed to create compliance standards for any company processing credit cards. Services like PayPal can perform the payment processing for online vendors, and has proven to be popular with online shoppers and businesses.

Chapter 4

SYSTEM ANALYSIS AND DESIGN

4.1 Use Case and Operation Contracts

The overall system consists of a Super Admin, any number of Managers and the general customers. The customer interacts with the system in two ways; either as a web customer or a registered customer. The web customer can view and browse the system and can register to get the other access to the system. The registered customer has a couple more access and permissions than the general web customer/user. The registered customer can view items, make purchase and check out to confirm their purchase. The system authenticates the registered users and provide them with access and permissions. The overall process can be depicted in the use case diagram below.

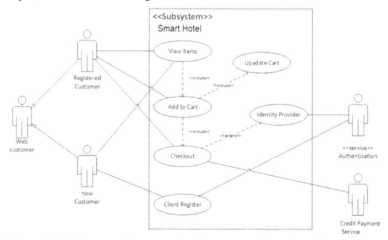

Figure 4- 1: Use case diagram for the user and system interaction.

The System Operation Contracts for above use case are depicted below:

Contract CO1: viewItems

Operation: viewItems ()

Cross references: use-case diagram for the user and system interaction

Preconditions: user browse the Page

Post conditions: list of items are displayed to the user

Contract CO2: addToCart

Operation: addToCart ()

Cross references: use-case diagram for the user and system
                     interaction

Preconditions: user select the menu items

Post conditions: -user adds item to the cart
                     -cart gets updated

Contract CO3: checkOut

Operation: checkout ()

Cross references: use-case diagram for the user and system

interaction, use-case diagram for user

Preconditions: user request for invoice.

Post conditions: none

Contract CO4: clientRegister

Operation: clientRegister ()

Cross references: use-case diagram for the user and system

interaction

Preconditions: user visits the web page for table register

Post conditions: -user scan the barcode from table into the system.

- **Super Admin**

Super Admin owes the overall control and responsibility to the system. The super admin has the prime right and access to the system. A super admin can add or remove features to the project or even has the complete right to discontinue or destroy the project. A super admin can add new manager or remove existing manager. He/she can permit necessary rights and authorities control to the manager. Super admin can even add, remove, verify or modify products, categories and users. The overall super Admin panel can be represented in the use case shown below.

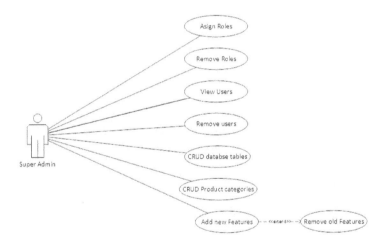

Figure 4-2: Use case diagram for Super Admin.

The System Operation contracts for Super Admin Use case are shown below:

Contract CO5: assignRoles
Operation: assignRoles ()
Cross references: use-case diagram Super Admin
Preconditions: must be super admin of the system
Post conditions: -assigns or revoke roles and permissions to or form users

Contract CO6: viewUsers
Operation: viewUsers ()
Cross references: use-case diagram Super Admin
Preconditions: must be super admin of the system
Post conditions: -search users from database view their details -removes user

Contract CO7: CRUD database tables

Operation: crudDbTables ()

Cross references: use-case diagram Super Admin

Preconditions: must be super admin of the system

Post conditions: -Create/Read/Update/Delete table to and from database

Contract CO8: CRUD product Categories

Operation: crudProductCategories ()

Cross references: use-case diagram Super Admin

Preconditions: must be super admin of the system

Post conditions: - Create/Read/Update/Delete product categories to and from the product table

Contract CO9: addNewFeatures

Operation: addNewFeatures ()

Cross references: use-case diagram Super Admin

Preconditions: must be super admin of the system

Post conditions: - add new features in the system

    - remove existing features from the system

- The Manager

The Manager is another actor of this project. Whenever the super admin creates a unique Manager, he/she is also assigned a set of authorities and access to the system.

The Managers are the people who runs small shops or firm with the goods that met the requirements of our site. A Manager can also be an individual person who locally produces and build Nepali goods and products. A Manager has the access to the system by logging in. The Manager can add item along with item details, remove items or modify products. Managers also delivers the product ordered by the customer and receive payment from them and update the inventory item.

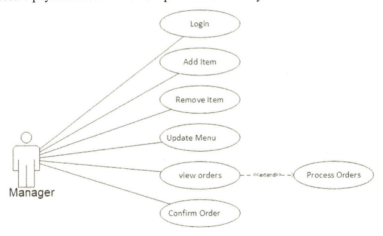

Figure 4- 3: use case diagram for Manager.

The System Operation Contracts for Manager Use case are shown below:

Contract CO10: addItem

Operation: addItem ()

Cross references: use-case diagram Manager

Preconditions: Manager logged into their account

Post conditions: item was added

Contract CO11: removeItem

Operation: removeItem ()

Cross references: use-case diagram Manager

Preconditions: item was added

Post conditions: item was removed

Contract CO12: updateMenu

Operation: updateMenu ()

Cross references: use-case diagram Manager

Preconditions: -Added/Remove Menu

Post conditions: changes were made in the inventory

Contract CO13: viewOrders

Operation: viewOrder ()

Cross references: use-case diagram Manager

Preconditions: -product(s) was ordered by customer

Post conditions: orders were viewed and processed

Contract CO14: confirmOrder

Cross references: use-case diagram Manager

Preconditions: -order was processed

Post conditions: - customer order was confirm

- The Registered User

Users can browse as guest on the site or register and login to get access to most of the features. A registered user can login into the system and order for items. The logged in user can view and order item and add to his/her cart or remove previously item added to the cart. He/she can checkout of the system to order and get total billing amount and logout of the system. The user does not have any permissions and authority to add or change any feature the system apart from ordering and browsing items and products.

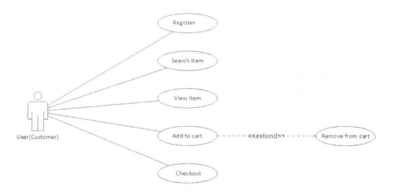

Figure 4- 4: use case diagram for Registered User

The System Operation Contracts for User use case are shown below

Contract CO15: register

Operation: register ()

Cross references: use case diagram user

Preconditions: none

Post conditions: new user was created

Contract CO17: searchItem

Operation: searchItem ()

Cross references: use case diagram user

Preconditions: none

Post conditions: searched item was displayed

Contract CO18: viewItem

Cross references: use case diagram user

Preconditions: item was searched

Post conditions: details of the particular item was displayed

---

Contract CO19: addToCart

Operation: addToCart ()

Cross references: use case diagram user

Preconditions: -item was searched

    -item was viewed

Post conditions: -item was added to the cart

    -user proceeded to checkout

4.2   Activity Diagram

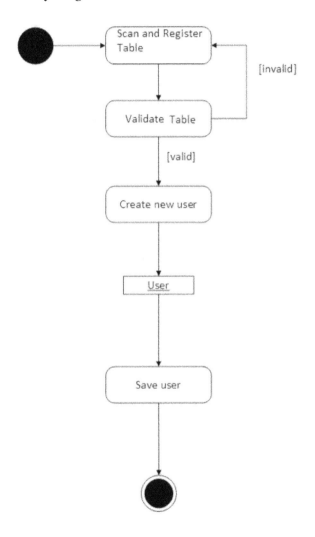

Figure 4- 5: Activity Diagram for User Registration.

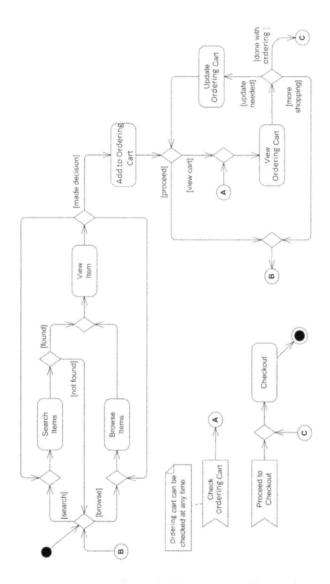

Figure 4- 6: Activity Diagram for Ordering.

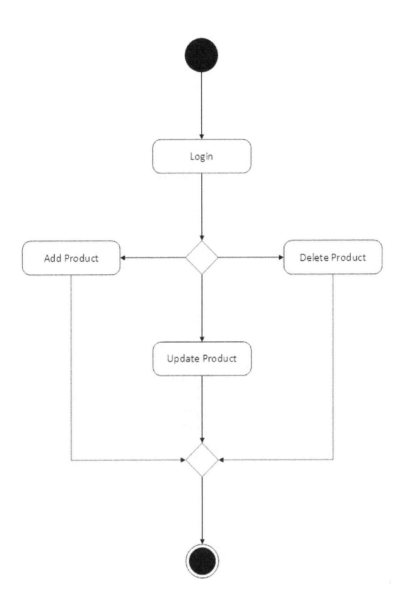

Figure 4- 7: Activity Diagram for Manage

29

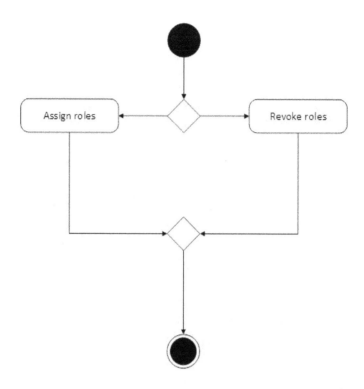

Figure 4- 8 : Activity Diagram for Super Admin User Roles Management.

4.3   Domain Model

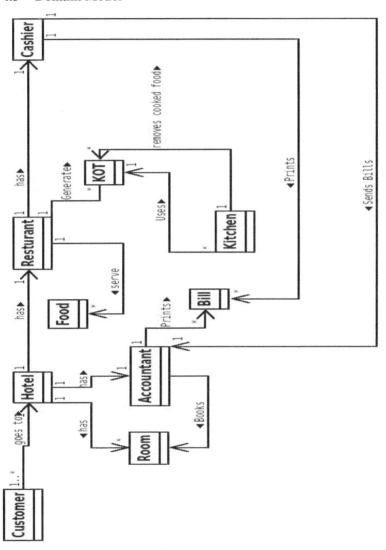

Figure 4- 9: Domain Model.

31

4.4   Entity-Relation (ER) Diagram

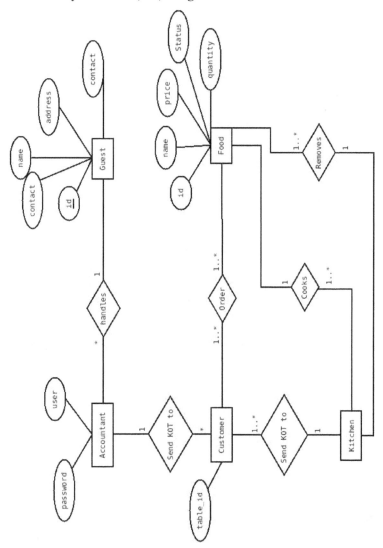

Figure 4- 10 : ER Diagram

4.5   System Sequence Diagrams

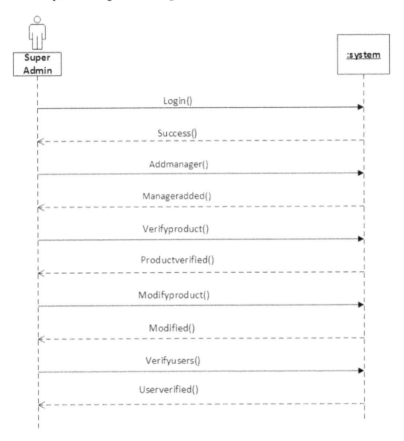

Figure 4- 11: SSD for Super Admin.

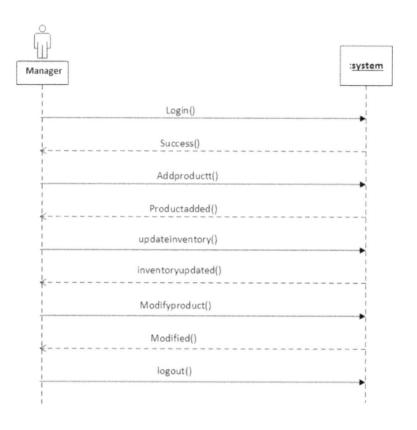

Figure 4-12: SSD for Manager.

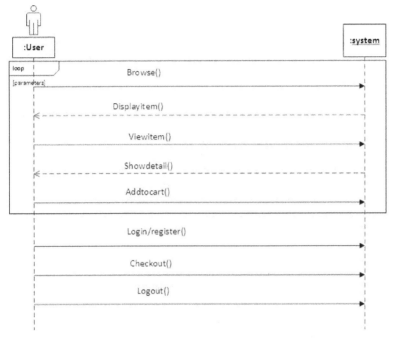

Figure 4- 13: SSD User(Customer).

4.6   Interaction Diagram (Sequence Diagrams)

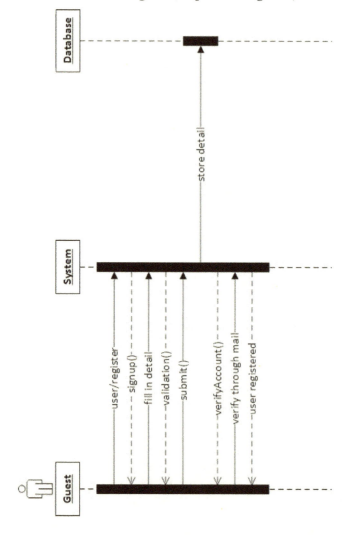

Figure 4- 14: Sequence Diagram for User Registration

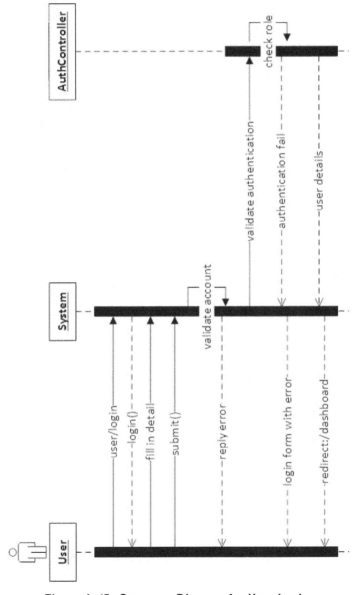

Figure 4- 15: Sequence Diagram for User Login.

37

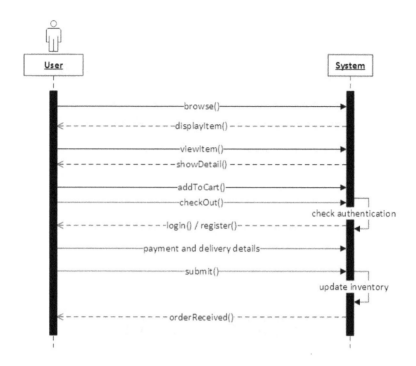

Figure 4- 76: Sequence Diagram for Shopping.

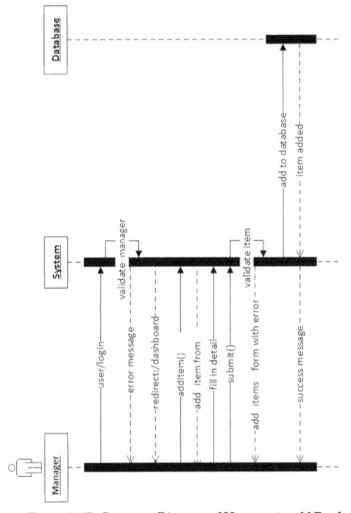

Figure 4- 17: Sequence Diagram of Manager to add Product.

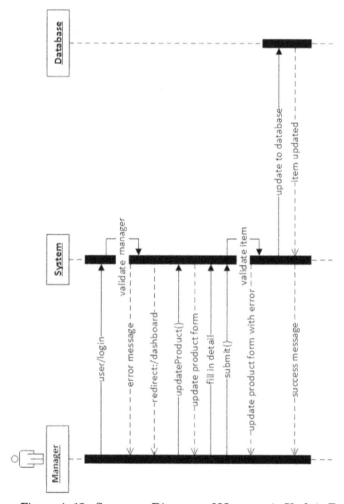

Figure 4- 18: Sequence Diagram of Manager to Update Product.

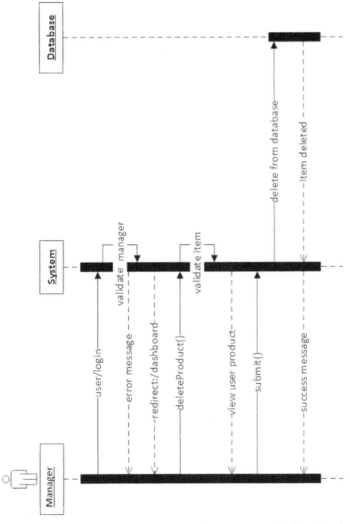

Figure 4-19: Sequence Diagram of Manager to Delete Product.

41

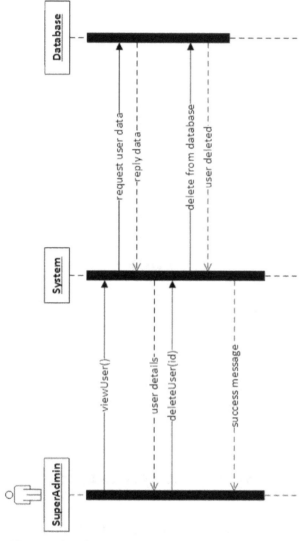

Figure 4-20: Sequence Diagram of Super Admin to view or delete user.

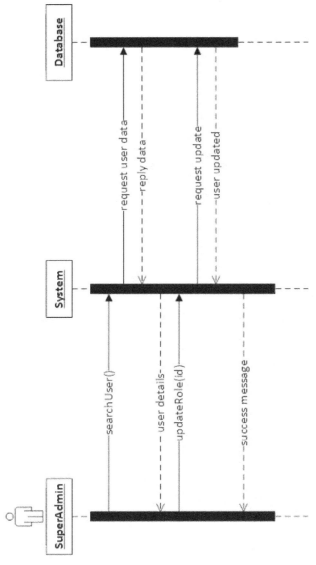

Figure 4-21: Sequence Diagram of Super Admin to assign/Revoke Roles

Chapter 5

TESTING

In this strategic testing, road map was drawn and testing was conducted.

5.1 Scope

The overall purpose of testing was to ensure that **Smart Restaurant** web application meets all of its technical, functional and business requirements. The purpose of this document is to describe the overall testing done for our website application. The approach described in this document provides the framework for all testing related to this application. Individual test cases were written for each version of the application that was released.

5.2 Test Objectives

The quality objectives of testing the Smart Restaurant web application were to ensure complete validation of the business and software requirements:

- Verify that software requirements are complete and accurate.
- Perform detailed test planning.
- Identify testing standards and procedures that will be used on the project.
- Prepare and document test scenarios and test cases.
- Regression testing to validate that unchanged functionality has not been affected by changes.
- Manage defect tracking process.
- Provide test metrics/testing summary reports.

5.3 Testing Goals

The goals in testing this application included validating the quality, usability, reliability and performance of the application. Testing was performed from a black-box approach, not based on any knowledge of internal design or code. Testing was done around requirements and functionality.

Another goal was to make the tests repeatable for use in regression testing during the project lifecycle, and for future application upgrades. A part of the approach in testing was to initially perform a 'Smoke Test' upon delivery of the application for testing. Smoke Testing is typically an initial testing effort to determine if a new software version is performing well enough to accept it for a major testing effort. For example, if the new software is crashing frequently, or corrupting databases, the software is not in a stable enough condition to warrant further testing in its current state. This testing was performed first. After acceptance of the build delivered for system testing, functions were tested based upon the designated priority (critical, high, medium, low).

5.4 What were tested

The following features of the website were tested for accuracy

- Home page
- Categories
- Items page
- Cart menu
- Checkout Process

5.5 Entrance Criteria

- All design specifications were reviewed and approved.

- Unit testing was completed by the development team, including vendors.

- All hardware needed for the test environment were available.

- The application delivered to the test environment were of reliable quality.

- Initial smoke test of the delivered functionality was approved by the testing team.

- Code changes made to the test site went through a change control process.

5.6 Exit Criteria

- All test scenarios were completed successfully.

- All issues prioritized and priority issues resolved.

- All outstanding defects were documented in a test summary with a priority and severity status.

- Go/No-go meeting were held to determine acceptability of product.

5.7 Test Execution

The test execution phase was the process of running test cases against the software build to verify that the actual results meet the expected results. Defects discovered during the testing cycle were introduced to the developers. Once a defect was fixed by a developer, the fixed code was incorporated into the application and regression tested.

These following testing phases was completed:

- Unit Testing

Unit testing was performed by the **Smart Restaurant** development team in their development environment. The developers knew and tested the internal logical structure of each software component.

- Functional Testing

Functional testing focused on the functional requirements of the software and was performed to confirm that the application operates accurately according to the documented specifications and requirements, and to ensure that interfaces to external systems are properly working.

- Regression Testing

Regression testing was performed to verify that previously tested features and functions do not have any new defects introduced, while correcting other problems or adding and modifying other features.

- Integration Testing

Integration testing was the phase of software testing in which individual software modules were combined and tested as a group. In its simplest form, two units that have already been tested were combined into a component and the interface between them was tested. In a realistic scenario, many units were combined into components, which were in turn aggregated into even larger parts of the program. The idea was to test combinations of pieces and eventually expand the process to test your modules with those of other groups. Eventually all the modules making up a process were tested together.

- Interface Testing

This testing followed a transaction through all of the product processes that interact with it and tests the product in its entirety. Interface testing were performed to ensure that the product actually works in the way a typical user would interact with it.

- Destructive Testing

Destructive testing focused on the error detection and error prevention areas of the product. This testing was exercised in an attempt to anticipate conditions where a user may encounter errors. Destructive testing was less structured than other testing phases and was determined by individual testers.

- User acceptance testing

User acceptance testing activities were performed by the business users. The purpose of this testing was to ensure the application meets the users' expectations. This also included focuses on usability and included appearance, consistency of controls, consistency of field naming, accuracy of drop down field information lists, spelling of all field name/data values, accuracy of default field values, tab sequence, and error/help messaging.

- Browser Testing

Functional and Regression as defined in this test strategy were executed using following Browsers:

- o Google Chrome
- o Microsoft Edge
- o Mozilla Firefox

5.8 Test Result

The test result of each unit test and integration test are done while developing the system and is reviewed to identify and remove errors. The

Following table consists of the test results of Black Box Testing which are performed to validate the system with respect to the requirement.

Id	Test	Expected Behavior	Precondition	Actual Behavior	Result
1.	Connect	User connect Wi-Fi of hotel	None	User connected to hotel network	Pass
2.	Register	The user should register	1 PASS	user registers by scan barcode of table	Pass
3.	Test register with already taken	Table no already taken error should be generated	None	As Expected	Pass
4.	Register with invalid barcode	Invalid error should be generated	None	As Expected	Pass
5.	Adding product to cart	Product with that product Id should be added to the cart using Session	None	As Expected	PASS
6.	Adding same product to cart	Adding same product in cart should only increase the quantity of the product not the product row.	5PASS	As Expected	PASS

50

7.	Reducing product from cart	reducing a product from cart should decrease the quantity of that certain product by 1 or by the amount deducted by the user along with the tax and grand total.	None	As Expected	PASS
8.	Remove all products from cart	All products rows should be removed and no carts should be shown and "No items in cart" should be shown.	7PASS	"No items in the cart" message is displayed	PASS
9.	Checkout form system	The user should be view the details of his order and can print out bill.	None	As Expected	PASS

Table 6-1. Test Results

51

Chapter 7
RESULT AND DISCUSSIONS

We started to develop this system as our Final Year Major Project for the Bachelor of Engineering Software Engineering. Within the time frame we submitted the proposal report for commencing this particular project. The project was completed within the given time frame with active involvement and coordination of all of the three team members and excellent support from the supervisor.

With the goal, which we started this project, we have come far ahead now where we can now start deploying our project in the market with a very little cost and effort.

Smart Restaurant is focused on providing a user-friendly and easy to use web application for people to order restaurants products. People can easily order their menu of hotel products. With a single user register by barcode in table.

Chapter 8

FUTURE IMPROVEMENTS

In the very first version of this project we have integrated a number of features and options. Being an ecommerce system, the need to improve and introduce new additional features and removal of some existing features is a must. So, for our next version we have planned and made plenty of research tasks to make our system much more advance. Some of the future improvements for this project can be listed below:

- Full hotel management system
- Advanced rating and review of individual products.
- Advanced reporting of unrelated bad products for the users to filter the products more precisely.
- Better recommendation systems to show related products based on user's products views, purchase etc.
- Enhanced recommendation system for users to recommend particular products to their relative and friends.
- Advanced compare sub system integration for users to go for the best choice on the spot.
- Social Media integration in the system for registration/login and sharing.

Chapter 9
CONCLUSION

Hence, our project will successfully complete to helps in increasing the opportunities in employment and uplifting the economic status of restaurant areas. It will not only help to order the products in our restaurant but also help to record the activities log which will help us to collect good revenue from Restaurant.

Smart Restaurant as a whole will make the process of online ordering in Restaurant. And the best part of all of this is that people will be able to search for the products in their own backyard. This will certainly help little or more for uplifting the Restaurant economy and their identity.

Bibliography

Fakhroutdinov,K. (2010). *http://www.uml-diagrams.org/examples/online-shopping-use-case-diagram-example.html*.Retrieved from http://www.uml-diagrams.org.

foodmandu.com.(2016).*http://foodmandu.com/*.\Retrieved from http://foodmandu.com/.

investopedia.com.(2015,10). *http://www.investopedia.com/terms/b/btob.asp*. Retrieved from http://www.investopedia.com.

investopedia.com. (2015, 03). *http://www.investopedia.com/terms/b/btoc.asp*. Retrieved from http://www.investopedia.com.

JetBrains. (2016). *https://www.jetbrains.com/phpstorm/*. Retrieved from https://www.jetbrains.com/phpstorm/.

Kaymu.com.np. (2015). *http://Kaymu.com.np*. Retrieved from http://Kaymu.com.np.

Khan, H. (n.d.). *A Report on eCommerce Trends in Nepal*. http://www.kaymu.com.np/.

Laravel. (2016). *https://laravel.com/docs/5.2*. Retrieved from https://laravel.com.

Larry Press, S. G. (n.d.). *Electronic commerce in Nepal*. Retrieved from https://www.isoc.org/:

https://www.isoc.org/oti/articles/0401/press.html

Products, N. (2015). *http://www.nepaliproducts.com/about_us.php*. Retrieved from http://www.nepaliproducts.com/.

Shop, N. A. (2007). *http://www.nepalartshop.com/*. Retrieved from http://www.nepalartshop.com/.

wikipedia. (2016, 11 16). Retrieved from https://en.wikipedia.org/wiki/Laravel.

wikipedia. (2016, 11 18). *https://en.wikipedia.org/wiki/JavaScript*. Retrieved from https://en.wikipedia.org: https://en.wikipedia.org/wiki/JavaScript

Wikipedia. (2016, 11 03). *https://en.wikipedia.org/wiki/Role-based_access_control*. Retrieved from https://en.wikipedia.org/wiki/Role-based_access_control.

YOUR KNOWLEDGE HAS VALUE

- We will publish your bachelor's and master's thesis, essays and papers

- Your own eBook and book - sold worldwide in all relevant shops

- Earn money with each sale

Upload your text at www.GRIN.com
and publish for free

www.ingramcontent.com/pod-product-compliance
Lightning Source LLC
La Vergne TN
LVHW092351060326
832902LV00008B/966